globe-
trotters
CLUB

Egypt

Tom Streissguth

🌿 Carolrhoda Books, Inc. / Minneapolis

Photo Acknowledgments

Photographs, maps, and artwork are used courtesy of: Laura Westlund, pp. 1, 2–3, 4, 20, 21, 25, 36–37, 39, 40, 45; Visuals Unlimited: (© Nada Pecnik) pp. 6, 19 (bottom), (© A.J. Cunningham) p. 9 (top); Middle East Pictures: (© Christine Osborne) pp. 7 (both), 8–9, 10 (both), 11 (top), 12, 13 (top), 15 (both), 16, 17 (both), 18, 20, 21, 22, 22–23, 23, 24, 26 (both), 27, 28, 29 (left), 30 (right both), 31, 32 (both), 33, 34, 35 (both), 38, 41 (both), 43, 44, (© Chris Barton) pp. 9 (bottom), 11 (bottom); © Michele Burgess, p. 13 (bottom); © Wolfgang Kaehler, p. 19 (top); © American Lutheran Church. Used by permission of Augsburg Fortress, p. 29 (right); Panos Pictures: (© Sean Sprague) p. 30 (left), (© Jean-Léo Dugast) p. 42; © Liba Taylor, p. 39. Cover photo of Luxor Temple, Middle East Pictures/© Christine Osborne.

Carolrhoda Books, Inc.
c/o The Lerner Publishing Group
241 First Avenue North
Minneapolis, Minnesota 55401 U.S.A.

Website address: www.lernerbooks.com

Words in **bold type** are explained in a glossary that begins on page 44.

Library of Congress Cataloging-in-Publication Data

Streissguth, Thomas, 1958–
    Egypt / by Thomas Streissguth
        p.   cm. — (Globe-trotters club)
    Includes index.
    Summary: An overview of Egypt emphasizing its cultural aspects.
    ISBN 1–57505–110–9 (lib. bdg. : alk. paper)
    1. Egypt—Juvenile literature. [1. Egypt.] I. Title II. Series:
Globe-trotters club (Series)
DT49.S87 1999
962—DC21   97–2700

Manufactured in the United States of America
1 2 3 4 5 6 – JR – 04 03 02 01 00 99

Contents

Misr Tura Hebu **Becum!***

*That's "Welcome to Egypt" in Arabic,
the official language of Egypt.

MEDITERRANEAN SEA

GAZA STRIP

WEST BANK

ISRAEL

JORDAN

Alexandria

Port Said

NILE DELTA

SUEZ CANAL

Ismailia

Suez

Giza

Cairo

QATTARA DEPRESSION

SIWAH OASIS

SAHARA

LIBYAN DESERT

Sinai Peninsula

Gulf of Suez

Jabal Katrinah ▲

Gulf of Aqaba

SAUDI ARABIA

EGYPT

DESERT

N

EASTERN

Nile River

DESERT

RED SEA

Luxor

Aswan

Lake Nasser

LIBYA

SUDAN

Legend

- 〰 mountains
- ⣿ deserts
- ▭ Nile Valley
- ★ capital city

Miles
0   50   100   150
0   100   200
Kilometers

Egypt occupies the northeastern corner of the continent of Africa. From the air, Egypt looks like a square, rock-covered beach. That's because the country is mostly **desert!** The Sahara Desert stretches across Egypt, from the country of Libya in the west to the Red Sea in the east. The desert crosses into Sudan, Egypt's southern neighbor.

Millions of green date palms grow on the coast between the brown Sahara Desert and the blue Mediterranean Sea, which borders northern Egypt. What's that green stripe connecting southern Egypt to the Mediterranean Sea? It's the valley created by the Nile River.

Slicing between the Sinai Peninsula and the rest of the country is the Suez Canal. This artificially constructed waterway lets ships sail between the Mediterranean Sea and the Gulf of Suez to the Red Sea, which links to the Indian Ocean. The eastern side of the Sinai Peninsula meets Israel and the Gulf of Aqaba.

Fast Facts about Egypt

Name: Jumhuriyat Misr al-Arabiya (Arab Republic of Egypt)
Area: 386,900 square miles
Main Landforms: Sahara Desert, Sinai Peninsula, Nile River
Highest Point: Jabal Katrinah (8,652 feet)
Lowest point: Qattara Depression (440 feet below sea level)
Animals: Gazelles, jackals, desert foxes, mountain sheep, crocodiles, scorpions
Capital City: Cairo
Other Major Cities: Alexandria, Aswan, Port Said, Suez, Ismailia
Official Language: Arabic
Money Unit: Egyptian pound

An Egyptian farmer (left) **guides his cattle along the banks of the Nile River, while a felucca** (facing page) **sails near Aswan. The Nile, which travels more than 4,000 miles across Africa, is the longest river in the world.**

Along the **Nile**

In Egypt daytime temperatures hover between 80 and 90 degrees in the summer and between 55 and 70 degrees in the winter. Desert highs can hit 110 in the afternoon and then sink close to freezing (32 degrees) after sunset.

You won't need a raincoat to keep dry in Egypt. In the southernmost areas, some kids have never seen rain. Each year about one inch of rain falls on Cairo, the country's capital. But along the Mediterranean coast, eight inches fall—that's a lot for Egypt!

The Nile River helps reduce the water shortage. For 960 miles of Egypt, the Nile runs through a green valley banked by cliffs and rocky hills. Where the river valley ends, the desert begins. And at its widest point, the valley is only about 10 miles across.

Egyptians need the Nile. Most of the people live near its banks and farm in the river valley. Egyptians

use the Nile's water to drink, to cook, to bathe, and to irrigate (water) their farms. People and goods travel the river on feluccas (sailboats), on modern motorboats, and on huge barges.

North of Cairo lies the Nile **Delta,** where the Nile fans into small rivers that travel to the Mediterranean Sea. Over the years, the Nile has brought fertile soil to the delta, where cotton and other **cash crops** thrive.

Holding Back the Nile

In the past, the Nile flooded every year. But these days, the Nile stays within its banks. In 1960 Egyptians began work on a dam at Aswan in southern Egypt. Finished in 1971, the Aswan High Dam created a huge lake called Lake Nasser. Egyptians named the dam after Gamal Abdel Nasser, the country's president from 1954 until his death in 1970.

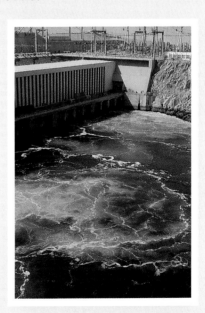

Dry Places and
Oases

 The Sahara Desert dominates Egypt's landscape. West of the Nile, the Sahara Desert is called the Libyan Desert. The Eastern (or Arabian) Desert is the part of the Sahara stretching from the Nile to the Red Sea. The Sinai Peninsula is desert, too. These spots are so dry that hardly any people live in them.

Small mountain ranges cover parts of the deserts and cross borders into Libya and Sudan.

Rocky hills stretch across the Eastern Desert. Rugged mountains and the country's highest point, Jabal Katrinah, lie on the Sinai Peninsula.

The mountains in Egypt rarely see rain, and empty riverbeds—known as **wadis**—line the slopes. When it does rain, the water floods the wadis. Other parts of the desert sink down like giant, empty lakes. Egypt's lowest point, the Qattara Depression, lies 440 feet below sea level. But it stays dry.

The Libyan Desert stretches as far as the eye can see. Although this sandy stretch of land looks pretty barren, the Bahariyya Oasis (facing page) **can support plants, animals, and people.**

Sandstorm

In springtime a hot wind called a khamsin sometimes blows from the south. When a khamsin is on the way, the temperature can soar 70 degrees in only a few hours. A brown cloud made of sand whips across the desert plains. Heavy dust and grains of sand as sharp as needles rain down from the sky, moving with such force that they can blast the paint off of a car. The storms can last for days.

In rocky parts of the desert, some stone has worn away to let underground water reach the surface. A large and steady spring can create a lush, green **oasis.** Some Egyptian oases support towns, farms, and forests of date palms. Thousands of people, for example, make their homes in Siwah Oasis, where farmers raise olives, oranges, and lemons.

Good **Fellahs**

About 65 million people populate Egypt. Most live near the Nile or along the Mediterranean coast. Half of all Egyptians make their homes in small rural villages. The government employs some people to work on huge cotton farms. But most rural people are *fellahin* (farmers) who own or rent a small plot of land near their village. A *fellah* (male farmer) and *fellaha* (female farmer) raise crops such as barley, rice, wheat, and cotton. Some fellahin tend groves of date palms and harvest the fruit. Others grow clover to feed their goats, pigeons, and chickens. Kids take care of the animals and help

Egyptian fellahin use both ancient and modern techniques to obtain water for irrigation. Some employ livestock to turn a water wheel (left), while others use gas-powered pumps (bottom).

harvest crops, but most children attend school during the day.

Egyptian farmers use the Nile to irrigate their fields. They dig canals and basins that the Nile's water fills. When the crops need water, workers open gates on the canals to let water flood the farmland.

That's really using your head! A group of fellaha carry home their crops after a hard day of work.

It's a Date!

Date palms love Egypt's hot weather. These trees can grow to be a hundred feet high! Their broad, feathery leaves provide shade and can be woven into items such as baskets and mats. The palms bear sweet fruit—called dates—that both people and animals like to eat. Egyptian cooks use them to flavor dishes. Mashed dates become a drink called *arak*. Egyptians also get sugar, fuel, and building material from these useful trees. Wow!

Most Egyptians are Hamitic Arabs. They are descendants of ancient Egyptians and the Arabian peoples who came to Egypt long ago.

Who Lives in
Egypt?

People have lived in Egypt for thousands of years. Ancient Egyptians probably came from southern Africa. In the seventh century A.D., people from the **Arabian Peninsula** began moving to **North Africa.** These days most Egyptians—80 percent—are **Hamitic Arabs.** They find both Arab people and the ancient Egyptians in their family tree.

The Nubians live in the southernmost part of Egypt and make up the country's second-largest **ethnic group.** Some Nubians tattoo blue patterns on their lips that show the

clan to which they belong. Desert dwellers, including the Bedouin, are smaller ethnic groups.

Members of different ethnic groups try to help one another out. In Egypt's harsh climate, life can be tough for everyone. So, everyone wants to lend a hand to a person in trouble.

A young Nubian rests on his felucca near Aswan.

Nomads

The Bedouin are nomads who travel across the country's deserts. Members of this group make their homes in large black goatskin tents. They herd small flocks of sheep, goats, and camels. When it's time to bring their flocks to market or to a new pasture, Bedouin pack up their tents and move. Camels help most nomads travel, but some Bedouin prefer to drive cars across the deserts. Many Bedouin have settled in towns and have stopped following the nomadic lifestyle.

Family Ties

In Egypt **extended families** are very close. Brothers, sisters, parents, and their other relatives depend on one another. If one member of a family loses a job or if another needs a hand repairing a house, the others help out if they can. Grandparents might guide grandchildren through their schoolwork. Cousins join one another in business. Aunts and uncles open their homes to nieces and nephews who need places to stay.

And when Egyptians get married, the families enjoy a big wedding. Some families rent rooms in fancy hotels. Rock bands or pop singers may perform. Other folks hold wedding parties in the streets of their village. Local musicians play and everyone eats a huge feast. After the wedding ceremony, guests might barrel around town in their cars, shouting, laughing, and honking their horns.

Newly married couples often live with the husband's family. Many Egyptian parents raise large families with four, five, or even more children. They believe that children help the family prosper and that kids with lots of sisters and brothers are happier. Grandparents, aunts, and uncles offer their advice and help raise children. Cousins grow up together, keeping Egyptian families close.

Tough Stuff

Life in Egypt can be hard. Modern medicine isn't easy to come by, so many Egyptians suffer from diseases. The Nile is polluted. Most kids leave school before they are 14 years old. Grown-ups have trouble finding jobs. And not all Egyptians can afford to buy enough food to feed their families. But all Egyptians, even very poor ones, share what they have.

Most Egyptian couples celebrate their wedding with lots of friends and family members.

All in the Family

Here are the Arabic words for family members. Practice using these terms on your own family! See if they can understand you!

grandmother	*jeddatee*	(ZHED-ah-tee)
grandfather	*jeddee*	(ZHED-ee)
mother	*omun*	(OH-moon)
father	*eb*	(EHB)
sister	*okht*	(OH-kit)
brother	*okh*	(OAK)
daughter	*bent*	(BINT)
son	*wuld*	(WILD)
aunt	*omti*	(AAHM-tee)
uncle	*omi*	(AAHM-ee)

Cairo is a huge city, filled with modern buildings, parks, and lots of people. The city is home to Egypt's government and to many big businesses.

Cairo

Cairo, a crowded, sprawling **metropolis** on the banks of the Nile, is Africa's biggest city. Founded more than a thousand years ago, Cairo is a mix of the modern and the ancient. People maneuver their cars alongside folks riding donkeys and horses that pull carts loaded with goods. Skyscrapers soar near old stone buildings that house shops and homes. Some Cairenes, as the city's residents are called, shop in modern supermarkets and department stores. Others prefer to buy items at marketplaces called souks.

Fifteen million people live in Cairo and its suburbs, so it's hard for everyone to find shelter. Several families may crowd into a single apartment or even a single room in a small house. Some Cairenes solve the problem by building small houses on rooftops. Newcomers might live in houseboats that float on the Nile. Well-off families have spacious apartments, but few have large houses.

All of Egypt's other large cities also lie near water. A busy port on the Mediterranean Sea, Alexandria is Egypt's second-largest city. It sits at the edge of the Nile Delta. Huge oceangoing ships dock at Port Said and Suez, Egyptian port cities on the Suez Canal. Aswan rises along the banks of the Nile, near Lake Nasser.

Although parts of Cairo are very modern, people still wash their clothes by hand in the narrow, crowded streets of the city's old section.

Mokattam Hill

The Mokattam Hill sits at Cairo's easternmost edge. Here live the *zabbaline,* the garbage collectors and recyclers of Cairo. They scour the city and a dump at the foot of Mokattam Hill for old cans, copper pots, glass bottles, old furniture, tools—anything that can be used again. The zabbaline sell the material to Cairo's factories and to workshops that can use the old stuff to make new articles.

Cool **House!**

In central Cairo, families live in small houses or in older apartment buildings. Wooden window screens let in light and air but keep out dust. Tall concrete apartment houses rise on Cairo's outskirts, away from the banks of the Nile.

In the countryside, Egyptian villagers build homes from bricks made out of mud, chopped-up straw, and water taken from the Nile. Most homes have a few rooms. After passing through an entrance hall, a family member or visitor enters a room that's both a living space and a kitchen. Here, the family might use a clay oven to prepare their food. Some cooks prefer outdoor ovens. In a smaller room, a *zeriba*, people might store food or shelter livestock. The house's small windows don't usually have glass—wooden shutters keep

Why Is a Ship Painted on that House?

Many families create murals (large wall paintings) on the front of their homes. Some murals depict interesting sites, animals, or Arabic letters and sayings. Others might show a ship, a train, or even an airplane to illustrate to viewers how a family traveled on a trip.

Egyptian villagers live a lifestyle similar to that of their ancestors. In this ancient village near the city of **Luxor** (left), **most of the houses are built with bricks made of mud and straw. Villagers use rooftops** (below) **as storage areas.**

out the sand. Many houses surround a courtyard, where residents can safeguard their animals at night.

Country homes have flat roofs where people can store crops or cooking fuel (cakes of dung, straw, or dried palms). Clay structures house pigeons, a favorite food, and tower from some rooftops. More often, though, the Egyptians build pigeon houses on the ground.

Speaking **Arabic**

Egyptians speak Arabic, which is also the official language of about 20 other countries in North Africa and on the Arabian Peninsula. In each country, Arabic sounds a little different, but most speakers understand the Egyptian version. That's because Egypt has the biggest film and TV industry of any Arabic-speaking land.

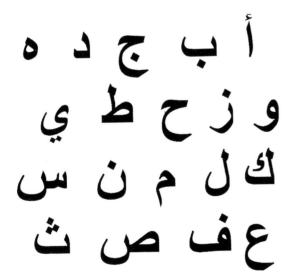

If you're reading this from left to right, you're going the wrong way! In Arabic writing goes from right to left.

Arabic Numbers

Numbers are written differently in the Arabic language. They're also pronounced differently. Here's how to pronounce some numbers in Arabic.

1	١	**WAH-hid**
2	٢	**it-NAYN**
3	٣	**tah-LAH-tah**
4	٤	**ar-BAH-ah**
5	٥	**KAHM-sah**
6	٦	**SIHT-tah**
7	٧	**SAHB-ah**
8	٨	**tah-MAHN-yah**
9	٩	**TIHS-ah**
10	١٠	**AH-shah-rah**

To say a number between 11 and 19, you say the single-digit number first, then add "ashar." For example, 13 would be "talatashar." Sixteen would be "sittashar."

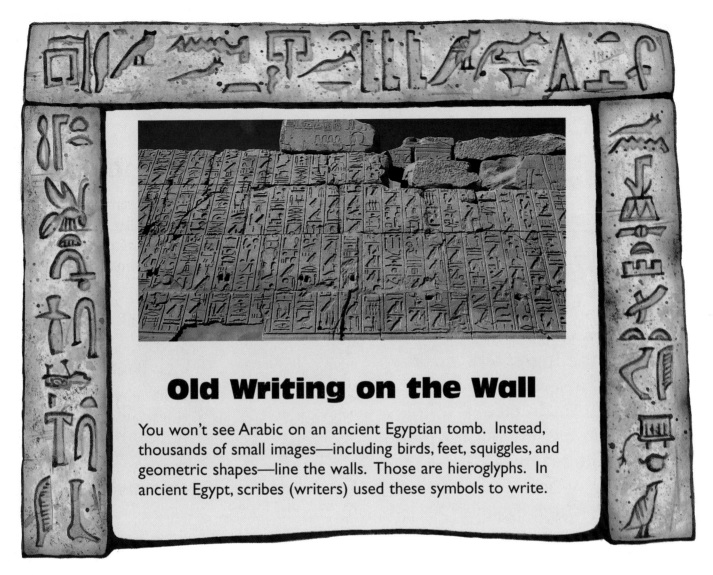

Old Writing on the Wall

You won't see Arabic on an ancient Egyptian tomb. Instead, thousands of small images—including birds, feet, squiggles, and geometric shapes—line the walls. Those are hieroglyphs. In ancient Egypt, scribes (writers) used these symbols to write.

Arabic is written from right to left across a page. Readers turn the pages of books and magazines from left to right. That's the opposite of the way people read and write in English! People write Arabic with two different alphabets. *Naskh* is used in books and newspapers. Most of the letters have squared-off shapes that make them easy to read. *Kufic* decorates pictures, the walls of mosques (houses of prayer), and book covers. Kufic letters have flowing, curving lines.

Mosques and
Minarets

Most Egyptians are Muslims, or followers of the religion of Islam. Muslims believe in one God, called Allah. Five times every day a **muezzin** heads to the top of a **minaret** (a tall, thin tower) and calls out, "Allah o akbar," which means "God is great." The cry lets Muslims know that it's time to pray.

When they can, Muslim men say their prayers at a mosque. Women usually pray at home. Mosques dot towns, cities, and the countryside in Egypt. When a Muslim man enters a mosque, he passes a walled courtyard. At a fountain in the center, he washes his hands, feet, and face. He leaves his shoes at the mosque's door. Inside, the floor is carpeted. Verses from the Koran (the Islamic holy book) appear in kufic script along the walls.

But not everybody can visit a mosque five times a day. Most Egyptian Muslims stop what they're doing and pray where they are—at work, outside, in a car, or at home.

Muslims try to visit the holy city of Mecca in Saudi Arabia, which lies west of Egypt on the Arabian Peninsula, at least once in their life. That's

A muezzin (facing page) **prepares to call Muslims to prayer from the top of a minaret. The Sultan Hussein Mosque** (left), **built in the 1300s, is one of the most famous in Cairo.**

Don't Look!

Some Egyptians believe in the evil eye—a menacing look that people worry might cause bad luck or unhappiness. In villages the skull of a crocodile sometimes glares from above a doorway. Its job is to keep away the evil eye.

where Muhammad, the founder of Islam, was born in the sixth century. Another important part of the Islamic religion is giving donations to the poor.

Some Egyptians follow other belief systems. Egyptian Christians are known as Copts. In their ceremonies, Copts use a language that helped scientists learn about the language of ancient Egypt.

Celebrate!

Egyptians love to celebrate important events. A festival called Sham al-Nasseem (that means "Scent of the Breeze") celebrates the arrival of spring. It's a favorite time for Egyptians to pack picnic lunches of onions, dyed eggs, and salted fish, which they enjoy at picnic spots like gardens and zoos.

Maoulid al-Naoubi marks the birthday of Muhammad and might last for as long as a week. In Ismailia, a large town on the Suez Canal, big tents fill the streets for the celebration. Inside the tent, Egyptians dance, bang drums, shake tambourines, and sing loudly. Jugglers, magicians, and fire-eaters per-

These young Muslims are joining in prayers during Id al-Fitr, a special festival that follows Ramadan.

Dear Grandpa,
Egypt is amazing! Today, we traveled along the Nile on a felucca. The wind was blowing hard, so we went pretty fast. Past the green farms along the Nile, I could see the reddish Sahara Desert. A kid I met told me that Egyptians call the desert the red land. They call the farmland near the Nile the black land, because that's the color of the soil. Neat!

I wanted to go swimming like some kids I saw, but the Nile is pretty polluted so I stayed on the boat. Tomorrow, we're going into the desert! I can't wait.

Love,
Nathan

form. Every night of the holiday, the town's residents join a parade that winds through the town. Similar celebrations are held all across Egypt.

Ramadan, the ninth month of the Islamic lunar (moon-based) calendar, is a special time for Muslims. During Ramadan, they eat a big breakfast, called *suhur*, before sunrise. Then Muslims fast (go without food) during the day. They don't drink, either! When the moon rises, it's time for a snack of dates or a glass of water. After praying at the mosque, the family shares a big meal, called *iftar*, at home.

Kids look forward to the first three days of the next month. That's Id al-Fitr, the Festival of Fast-breaking. People visit their friends and relatives, bringing sweets and other treats.

Young Egyptians head to classes at a primary school in the town of Luxor (above left). **Teachers and students** (above) **in Egyptian secondary schools take education very seriously.**

What a **Crowd!**

Kids cram into Egypt's schools. Because there are so many students, seats, desks, books, and teachers are in short supply. In Cairo some schools work in shifts—as many as three each day. The school stays open from early morning until late in the evening. Classrooms are places to be quiet and obedient. But at lunchtime, kids pass around sandwiches and fruit as they chat and joke.

Youngsters begin school at age six. After sixth grade, kids attend preparatory school (junior high) for three years. Lots of kids leave after preparatory school to take jobs. But some go on to secondary (high) school. The biggest university in Egypt is in Cairo. It's free to attend, so thousands of young people from Arabic-speaking countries crowd the campus. Another way to learn is by watching television. The Egyptian government airs educational programs. Kids who want to be engineers might watch the math lessons.

Street Writers

In the street near an Egyptian post office, men sit at small desks. People hand them papers, the men write on them and hand the papers back. The customers pay them a coin or two. What's going on? These men are scribes! Many Egyptian adults—about half—can't read or write. So a scribe does their writing for them.

Cairo University attracts students from all over the Arab world.

Souk **Shopping**

Most towns in Egypt have a souk (a marketplace). Whether held inside a huge building or out of doors, souks are noisy places full of laughing and bargaining.

Inside the souk, shoppers can find food or goods. Egyptian culture values generosity, so bakers let shoppers sample freshly baked bread. The smell of roasting meat fills the air.

One lane of the souk might be lined with the tiny stores of rug sellers or tent makers. In another street, metalsmiths sell copper pans, brass trays, or silver jewelry. In a certain area of the souk, shoppers can browse in a sweet-smelling row of spice shops.

Window Shopping

In Cairo and in Egypt's other cities, merchants push small carts around the neighborhoods. The carts, like shops on wheels, offer fruits, vegetables, bread, or fresh fish. Buyers lower a basket from their second-story window to the merchant, who pops his goods into the basket. The food goes up, and the payment comes back down.

A vendor at a souk in Cairo displays large bags of dates for shoppers. Sometimes vendors offer their customers a free taste.

If you shop at a souk, you won't see a price tag! Buyers and sellers must bargain over prices. They often share a cup of hot, sweet coffee while they reach an agreement. It can take a long time, and that's the way Egyptians like it. In a souk folks are hardly ever in a hurry.

Attention Camel Shoppers!

The Gimal market in Cairo is packed with people buying and selling camels. Why would anybody buy a camel? Because these animals are tough enough to walk through the desert carrying a heavy load or a rider. Some camels can also go all winter in the Sahara without a drink of water. Camels are nicknamed the ships of the desert because of their bobbing, rolling walk and their stamina.

Egyptian **Style**

In the countryside, Egyptian men wear the galabiah, a long, straight robe usually made of light cotton. A galabiah has a wide neck opening and long, wide sleeves. A woman's version of the galabiah looks pretty much the same. These lightweight outfits keep people cool in the hot sun. Egyptians have favored these outfits for thousands of years, but

Most Egyptians wear something on their head to protect against the sun. Some men wear skull caps (top), while others favor turbans (above). **Many Egyptian women** (left) **cover their heads with scarves.**

these days some people wear T-shirts underneath. Galabiahs can be any color but most wearers choose white, tan, or black.

In the cities, Egyptian men might choose shirts, trousers, and jackets. Women may dress up in blouses and skirts. All over Egypt, children go barefoot, while most adults put on sandals.

For headgear an Egyptian man might wind a long length of cloth around his head to make a turban. Others choose small cloth hats called skullcaps. Many Egyptian women wear scarves over their hair. A woman might put on a long dress and a veil that cover most of her body and head—even her face. Only her eyes peep through.

Desert Fashion

The Bedouin wear several layers of very lightweight robes, usually black or dark in color. Those outfits look hot, right? Actually, the layers of cloth let air move around and cool down the wearer. The layers also protect desert dwellers from the burning sun and the blistering wind, which can dry out or damage their skin.

A hearty bowl of *faoul* (left) served with pita bread is a staple of the Egyptian diet. An Egyptian woman pulls hot pita bread from a clay oven (below).

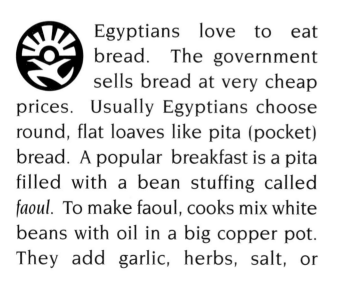

A *Faoul* for
Falafel

Egyptians love to eat bread. The government sells bread at very cheap prices. Usually Egyptians choose round, flat loaves like pita (pocket) bread. A popular breakfast is a pita filled with a bean stuffing called *faoul*. To make faoul, cooks mix white beans with oil in a big copper pot. They add garlic, herbs, salt, or lemon juice to give faoul a special flavor. Faoul is also tasty served with yogurt, cheese, or eggs.

Shops close for a few hours during lunch, which Egyptians like to eat in the middle of the afternoon. Cooks grill chunks of lamb on skewers with tomatoes, onions, peppers, and spices. Others roast pigeons stuffed with rice.

Other dishes round out the meal. Tahini (a paste of ground sesame seeds), *baba ganouche* (a mixture of tahini and eggplants), and *kochari* (a dish made with pasta, rice, lentils, and tomato sauce) are popular. Egyptians sometimes end lunch with fresh fruit.

At dinnertime, Egyptians like to eat falafel—balls of fried bean paste mixed with pepper, garlic, green onion, parsley, and other spices. Falafel makes a tasty stuffing for pita bread. Cooks add tomatoes or other vegetables to make the dish even more delicious.

Hummus

Let's make hummus, a dip that Egyptians love to eat with pita bread!

You will need:
1 can chickpeas (garbanzo beans)
2 cloves garlic, finely chopped
1 ½ teaspoons salt
2 lemons
½ cup tahini

Mash the chickpeas into a thick paste. You can use a spoon, a potato masher, or, with an adult's assistance, a food processor. Next, juice both lemons. Then add the lemon juice, salt, garlic, and the tahini to the chickpeas. Mix it all up with your spoon or food processor. Chill, and serve!

Hint: Tahini comes in cans and jars. It can be found in the foreign-food section of most grocery stores and in Middle Eastern food stores.

Pharaohs and Pyramids

Ancient history is everywhere in Egyptian cities such as Giza, Aswan, and Luxor. Thousands of years ago, pharaohs (kings) ruled Egypt. They ordered their subjects to build large stone buildings in the shapes of pyramids as royal tombs (graves). Most of the four-sided structures held a mummy (the preserved remains) of a pharaoh, as well as valuable treasures.

The Great Pyramid stands about 450 feet high at Giza, which is near Cairo. About 4,500 years ago, a very powerful pharaoh named Khufu had thousands of workers set rows of **limestone** blocks into the shape of the pyramid. Long ago the heavy blocks were covered with a white stone that glittered in the sun. Later Egyptians paved their roads using this white covering.

The Great Pyramid at Giza is the largest of Egypt's pyramids. This structure was built with two million limestone blocks, each weighing more than two tons. That's some heavy lifting!

Making a Mummy

Pharaohs and other important ancient Egyptians were mummified after they died. Ancient Egyptian priests used hooks to pull the dead person's brain out through the nose. After removing the organs, the priests soaked the body in natron (a kind of salt) to dry it out, then wrapped it in linen. Priests popped artificial eyes into the head and painted makeup on the face. Next, they lay the mummy in its coffin. Food, tools, furniture, and other personal items were placed in the tomb, too. Ancient Egyptians believed that these goods would help the pharaoh in the afterlife.

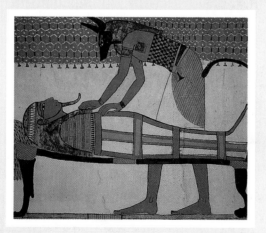

Ancient Egyptians believed that the Great Sphinx, a statue with a human head and a lion's body, would protect the pharaohs buried inside the pyramids. Over the years, wind and sand have eroded many of the sphinx's features.

A narrow, dark, and stuffy passage leads people far inside the Great Pyramid. High above rise more than two million blocks of limestone. At the pyramid's center is a burial chamber that was robbed of its treasure and its mummy long ago.

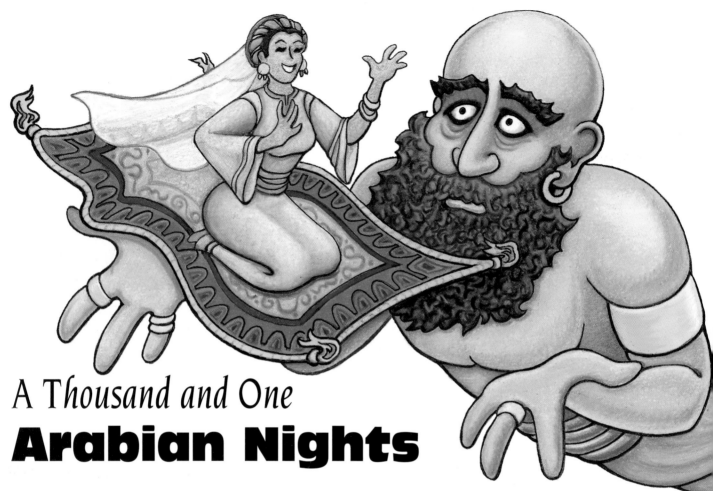

A Thousand and One
Arabian Nights

Have you ever heard of Aladdin? Or Sinbad? That means you know a story from A *Thousand and One Arabian Nights.* Many experts agree that a Cairene first wrote down these ancient stories. A manuscript fragment found in Egypt is about a thousand years old!

This Cairene compiler wasn't the person who made up the stories, which historians believe many people gathered together. But one legend says that a woman named Scheherazade was the first person to tell them. Here's the scoop.

A sultan (king) married a woman whom he loved very much. When the sultan discovered that his bride favored his cook, the sultan had his wife's head cut off. After that, the sultan decided to marry a woman every night and to have her beheaded the next day. His chief adviser hated the job of delivering the unlucky women to the sultan. After several years, he could keep the terrible secret no longer. He told his daughter Scheherazade.

The adviser regretted his decision, because Scheherazade married the sultan the next day. But she had a plan. She told the sultan a wonderful story that night. At the most exciting point, she stopped and only agreed to finish the tale the next night. In this way, she survived a thousand nights by telling tales of flying carpets, genies, treasure-filled caves, and magic lamps. On the 1,001st night, the sultan told Scheherazade that he loved her too much to harm her. Whew!

Author! Author!

In 1988 Naguib Mahfouz, a Cairene, became the first author who writes in Arabic to win the Nobel Prize for Literature. His books tell of life in modern and ancient Egypt.

Fun and
Games

After school kids help their families by doing chores. But most find time for fun. To cool off, youngsters might swim in the Nile or in the Mediterranean Sea. Kids in Egypt get a kick out of soccer. They play in the streets or on teams. Most kids don't have a soccer ball, but that's okay! Players make their own by filling a sock with sand. Fans can watch professional teams at a stadium near Cairo that seats 100,000 people.

Other kids play *seega*, an Egyptian version of tic-tac-toe. To play seega, two people draw a grid pattern in the ground. They each carry a small bunch of game pieces, which can be pebbles, polished stones, marbles, or even coins. The players place their markers down one at a time. The object of the game is to

Whether in the city or the countryside, Egyptian kids love to play soccer (above). **Seega** (facing page), **another popular game, has been played in Egypt for centuries.**

make a straight line of three stones. They can move their stones to a different square, one or two away. But a player can't jump an opponent's piece.

Meet Ezzat!

Ezzat is 10 years old. He lives with his three uncles, an aunt, some cousins, his parents, and his little sister in the large village of Om Khenan. Every morning he feeds his pet goat before he heads off to school. In the afternoon, Ezzat likes to play soccer with his friend Mohamed and other neighborhood kids. He's also on his school's soccer team. Can you guess Ezzat's favorite pastime?

Lights! Camera! **Action!**

Egypt has a thriving movie business that makes more than a thousand films each year—more than any other country in Africa! Moviegoers in many Arabic-speaking countries enjoy Egyptian films. Many of the movies are action films. Others are about family conflicts or romance. Some feature tales of ancient Egypt, with actors in fancy historical costumes.

But Egypt's government has strictly forbidden showing movies that say bad things about Egypt. Filmmakers aren't supposed to depict poverty or dishonest government officials.

Egyptians who own televisions watch soap operas, comedy programs, and thrillers. But when it is time for Muslims to pray, broadcasters remind people of their religious duty.

Shadow Puppets

Egyptians of all ages like to watch shadow puppet shows. Puppeteers move the puppets with strings or sticks. The puppets' shadows can be seen through a white screen. These plays usually have funny characters and lots of jokes. Some of the plays were first performed 700 years ago. Wow!

Giant movie posters (left) advertising the latest action flick or romance story can be found all over Cairo. If Cairenes don't have a television at home, they can always join a group of friends to watch TV at a café (below).

Egyptians don't have to own a VCR to watch a good video. Some people own a special electronic device that can send a movie playing on one VCR to any TV nearby.

The Arab Nightingale

Music is everywhere in Cairo, and many villagers listen to radios and recordings. Madonna and other rock musicians are well known in Egypt. Traditional Egyptian music sounds very different. Worshipers sing at mosques, farmers sing while they work, and boaters sing as they glide down the Nile. Street musicians may play stringed instruments, such as the lute and the *rebab* (fiddle), while others pipe on flutes.

Um Kulthum was an Egyptian singer whose real name was Fatima Ibrahim. Her nickname was the Arab Nightingale because her voice was as beautiful as the song of the nightingale. Um Kulthum's songs are usually slow paced, with traditional Egyptian instruments playing in the

Street musicians in Cairo entertain people with songs played on homemade instruments.

Café Life

Egyptians like to hang out at cafés, where they meet friends, play games of backgammon or dominoes, and listen to music. Most visitors sip strong, sweet coffee. Others choose *karkade*, a purple tea made from hibiscus flowers. Another option is mint tea served in glasses filled with boiling hot water and mint leaves. Cafés offer soft drinks called *kukula* and *bips*. What are those drinks called in English?

(Hint: Say them out loud. Do they sound familiar?)

Answer: Coca-Cola and Pepsi.

background. Some of her songs last for more than an hour! When she died in 1975, people filled Cairo's streets to attend her funeral.

Some Egyptian radio stations play only Um Kulthum's music, which also is featured in movies and on television programs. There are cafés in Cairo where visitors can spend an entire day sipping tea or coffee while listening to the songs of the Arab Nightingale.

Hold on to your hat! An Egyptian family enjoys a motorcycle trip through Cairo.

Glossary

Arabian Peninsula: A peninsula in southwestern Asia bordered by the Red Sea, the Persian Gulf, the Arabian Sea, and the Gulf of Aden (all of which belong to the Indian Ocean).

cash crop: A crop grown mainly to make money.

clan: A group of families who have a common ancestor.

delta: An area where a river branches into many channels before reaching its mouth.

desert: A dry, sandy region that receives low amounts of rainfall.

ethnic group: A large community of people that shares a number of social features in common such as language, religion, or customs.

extended family: Mothers, fathers, brothers, sisters, grandparents, aunts, uncles, and cousins who may share one household.

Hamitic Arab: A person with ancestors from both the Arabian Peninsula and ancient Egypt.

limestone: A kind of rock created by shells or coral being compressed for thousands of years.

metropolis: A large, important city.

minaret: A prayer tower built inside or beside a mosque.

muezzin: A crier who lets Muslims know when it is time for them to pray.

North Africa: A region of the African continent that includes Morocco, Algeria, Tunisia, Libya, and Egypt.

oasis: A fertile place in the desert that benefits from an underground water source.

wadi: A canyon or dry river channel that floods during rainstorms.

Flag

In 1952 a military group overthrew King Farouk, Egypt's ruler. The next year, the country became a republic—a country governed by elected officials. Egypt soon adopted a flag to reflect this change. A red stripe represents blood shed in the 1952 revolution. White symbolizes Egypt's bright future. A black stripe reminds Egyptians of life before the republic. The eagle is an Islamic symbol.

Pronunciation Guide*

Allah	AH-lah
Allah o akbar	AH-lah OH ahk-BAHR
al-Qahirah	ahl–kah-HEER-ah
faoul	FOWL
Farouk	fah-ROOK
fellah	FEH-lah
fellaha	fell-ah-HAH
fellahin	fell-ah-HEEN
hummus	HUH-muhs
iftar	ihf-TAHR
Islam	ihs-LAHM
khamsin	hahm-SEEN
Koran	koh-RAHN
kufic	koo-FEEK
Mecca	MEHK-kah
misr tora hebu becom	MAH-sir toh-RAH HEE-boo beh-KUM
muezzin	myoo-EH-zihn
Muslim	MOOS-lihm
Naguib Mahfouz	nah-GEEB mah-FOOZ
naskh	nuhs-KEH
Ramadan	RAH-mah-dahn
Scheherazade	Sheh-har-ah-ZAHD
seega	see-GAH
souk	SOOK
suhur	soo-HOOR
zabbaline	zeh-BAH-leen
zehriba	zehr-ee-BAH

*Pronunciations are approximate.

Further Reading

Arnold, Helen. *Postcards from Egypt*. Austin, TX: Steck Vaughn, 1996.

Bennet, Olivia. *A Family in Egypt*. Minneapolis: Lerner Publications Company, 1985.

Egypt in Pictures. Minneapolis: Lerner Publications Company, 1989.

Haskins, Jim. *Count Your Way Through the Arab World*. Minneapolis: Carolrhoda Books, Inc., 1991.

Heinrichs, Ann. *Egypt: Enchantment of the World*. Danbury, CT: Children's Press, 1997.

King, David C. *Egypt: Ancient Traditions, Modern Hopes*. New York: Marshall Cavendish, 1997.

Loveridge, Emma, *Egypt*. Austin, TX: Steck Vaughn, 1997.

Pitkanen, Matti A. *The Children of Egypt*. Minneapolis: Carolrhoda Books, Inc., 1991.

Polk, Milbry. *Egyptian Mummies: A Pop-Up Book*. New York: Dutton Books, 1997.

Tenquist, Alastair, *Egypt: Economically Developing Countries*. New York: Thomson Learning, 1997.

Wilcox, Charlotte. *Mummies and their Mysteries*. Minneapolis: Carolrhoda Books, Inc., 1993.

Metric Conversion Chart

WHEN YOU KNOW:	MULTIPLY BY:	TO FIND:
teaspoon	5.0	milliliters
Tablespoon	15.0	milliliters
cup	0.24	liters
inches	2.54	centimeters
feet	0.3048	meters
miles	1.609	kilometers
square miles	2.59	square kilometers
degrees Fahrenheit	5/9 (after subtracting 32)	degrees Celsius

Index